by

cold

water

T0072259

by
cold
water

poems
by
chris
dombrowski

wayne
state
university
press
detroit

Library of Congress Cataloging-in-Publication Data

Dombrowski, Chris, 1976–

   By cold water : poems / by Chris Dombrowski.

      p. cm. — (Made in Michigan writers series)

   ISBN 978-0-8143-3422-5 (pbk. : alk. paper)

   I. Title.

   PS3604.O453B9 2009

   811'.6—dc22

                              2008035496

   ∞

michigan council for
arts and cultural affairs

This book is supported by the Michigan Council for Arts and Cultural Affairs

Designed and typeset by Omega Clay

Composed in Neue Sans

These
poems
are
for
Mary

CONTENTS

by

cold

water

To Carry Water

There is the bird beak's way
and the way of the woman with child.

The eye's way
and the way of the well bucket.

The oak tree's way is not unlike that
of the cloud or the long dry summer it was

when the birdsong stopped,
and the woman stood tiptoe

looking down the well. Perched
on the handle of an unstrung pail, a wren

fluttered its wings without note. A leaf
floated, sinking slowly as the pail:

the rust holes, the caterpillar-chewed,
sipping in the weight of last year's skies.

For a moment of months, the woman is
the well—until the sky inside her

opens, and she stands above
holding a bucket full of leaf-song,

of wren-beak rain drops, of clouds
staring up like eyes.

Get Up, John

Here comes dawn and nothing rosy
about her fingers—stove-flame
blue and some hand must've turned
the burner on: the little tongues
licking, gradually, the teapot of us
aboil, cooking off a giardia
of stars, the dregs of our night-
mares. Who will place his fingers
in the nailmarks, come near enough
to smell death in its hair? Already we've
some of us slid back into our bodies,
restirring the air our breaths stirred
all night—whoever we are while
we sleep—and gone about believing
we are here. Ambulance sirens
assure us, a plum's sour skin, what's become
of the poppies, dried all but greenless,
et cetera. But the yearling child
reaching into the lineaments of sun
lancing between his crib bars—how might
this shame us, that they seem
to seem graspable to him?

Bullethole

In the window of the homestead, west window,
some bored son's .22. And peering out you feel

the slightest breeze tickle past an eyelid
and reach a cornea that can't see where dawn

(barely shooting light) comes from, can't see
the shots or echoes banking down the field—

but see how the dark disappears: fog draining
from the hunter-laden draws, funneling through

bottomland where creeks fall from pool
to dream. Follow that wind from its beginnings

in bluegrass, past the juncos' joust and scatter,
the dew-soaked fence posts, across County Road 664

down which a young man must have walked one day
and taking aim at his watery reflection, fired

once, though this morning wind arrives
as from a girl who once leaned over you, and blew

on your face to wake you: Key West, you were
just eighteen, trying to run your mother's heart

into the ground, and waking saw the eyes
of the past and the future staring down:

Where will you go, they asked, this is
everywhere, now.—Here, the determined

gaze holding yours demands, with what words,
how will you reconcile memory and sight:

What can you possibly say?

Fragments with Dusk in Them

We were taught to count kestrels on wires
like coins in our pockets. Whole years

we recalled by color: that torch-year,
tanager, fox, sandstone, sage. Droughts

revealed the river's former ways, oars wedged
between boulders, a derailed boxcar,

conductor's leather cap. A recluse fell in love
with certain shadows spilled across

her cellar floor, and among the east's first stars
were the occasional words jeweling-up at dusk

with junkyards, chrome hubcaps—as mirrors
struck small skies across our bodies.

October Suite

Old dog October arrives
half blind and wheezing,
limping its track
through ruts along the road.

I want to be worthy
of this waking dream:
my mother, before my birth,
kneads clouds at the counter.
Floured, rain-scent thick
as balm, they rise
in the far room and feed
no one. My father
walks the market, buys
hollow loaves, calls them
little worlds, little nothings.

First hike after the fires,
grasshoppers black
as burn. *Go on, hopper,*
fly away somewhere.
In the trees the scorched
knots look like people
clutching one another.

Tighten your purse strings,
my mother used to say,
your mouth is what you spend.
What if we learned to treat
each other as if a music
were barely playing?

To go to bed dusty
as unlit chandeliers,
and imagine it arriving
in a different season.
I used to think: December,
a windless day, bouncing
along the riverbottom until
an oak limb snags me,
swings me under
a shelf of ice . . . But this
is the only time of year
and this the only cloud:
it sweeps the sky like a sheet
snapped from a clothesline.
We stand beneath
the burial of this light
lifting hands to whatever
we lift hands to. And like a tack,
the near-full moon pins
a black note to the ridge.

Poem Beginning and Ending with Haiku

Deep rain. A starling grasps
the gutter. This morning reading
in my notes Issa's *Here, I'm here—*
snow falling! I thought for a moment
the words were mine. How to claim
his solitude, to inhabit that house
of phantom dwelling? In the year
of his life he bathed his son, second son,
and daughter Sato. Then Kiku, young wife
for whom he wrote *Chrysanthemums*
don't care what they look like, pregnant
again, fell ill and died, her infant son
following close behind. Dew drops,
dreams of melons, wild pink breaking
into scarlet flowers they used to pick. *A bath*
when you're born, a bath when you die,
he wrote, *how stupid*. Now the new rain
drips from the plastic flamingo's beak into
this garden, and the little girl tiptoeing
down the driveway, barefoot, out to get
her mother's mail, explains things.

Boreal

This time of year, when the sky is so much like a trough
we drink from by the day that goes on reflecting
itself and not the tired row of horses we are
nudging our way to water, our heads between the planets'
pewter light, the moot glow of stars,

                                             we forget things
we should remember: the barefoot feeling of walking
across a heel-mooned softwood floor; sunlight trapped
in shattered glass so bright it seemed the cause; a niece
who asked her uncle "will you be alive next fall?"

This time of year, a cloud is a cross, dawn is a hoof; the fir
a threadbare sail nightwinds needle through. Soon
we'll say the leaves are turning and stand in doorways,
necks upturned at flocks of geese, leaves at our feet
shuffling, as if there were somewhere to go.

One of the things I love about horses is how little I know
about them. I know a chestnut from a bay from a palomino
but beyond that I just say, beautiful horses, and know what I mean
when a twitch turns a mane to a shower of light,

when a stocking-footed mare stamps the hard ground
as if to say, this is what you have, the time
it takes to drop this hoof to dirt.

Midst

Apparitional   the mountains   in and out of mist
frame us   and the long curtains of water
falling   how far   to water coursing over
scattered mountain   a single heron gliding
through the heron-colored sky toward a stand of cottonwoods and rookery
fashioned from cottonwood branches   four more birds
from the neck up   the crags coming closer
in the fog   closer still in water
whose stillness   and our composition on it   is illusion
rife with light   how far back from it must we step
to see ourselves   as we are seen   here
shapes   moving within moving frames

Some Nights the River

Some nights the river draws
a line with itself in ice.
                          I could forgive you that far, but twice and I'd
have to—
                Trace: the moon-drafted aspen branch on snow.
Lighter charcoal. Don't press so hard. I never learned
to shade.
                Could you draw it in the dark?—answer me.
                                              He was
sour: the band had dumped him 'cause they didn't like
his shuffle: But I could draw your shoulder.
                                    That one.

        *

Before this, there is the small, still-forming body
                                    inside a larger body—
and before that, the river, the trees, the man and the woman—
running a hand (small, still-forming) across its world's firmament
so that the being-holding body, choke-picking,
                                    quivers as leaves do
when there is no wind,
                only the expectation of it,
                                    and thinks, *light begets light,*
but doesn't write it down.

        *

The scrawl on the railcar—(the train had slowed
at a crossing) "I love the whole world!"—was moving
too fast usually for anyone to protest.

                            The carpenter'd come outside, piss
a whole novel's worth of characters in the snow.

                                 Stick-figures but still
they'd start to tell a story. And soon enough it'd thaw.

                                 (Omit.
Wanted to say too much.)

                    Back when I was mascoting for the Osprey,
on the last day of the season once, early fall, a live osprey
hung plumb over the stadium,

                        big trout flapping in its talons.
When we rose to our feet cheering, the bird
fumbled the fish, then swooped down,
caught it by the tail.

                  That, he said, snapping a faint line of chalk
across the new foundation, *will never happen again.*

    *

First at first light the crabapple,

                        Tom Sawyering the aspens and volunteer maples,
scribing itself on the fence.

                  Then the whole grove.

                          That's
my nose? That's not my nose. He loved her like the horizon
and she acted the part: come toward her, she'd take one
long step back.

Two crows rowing through the rain—where does their wave
hit shore?

*

The affair came first as notion
then as murmur,
next as a lump in the throat.
Soon a gaff, a May river unfordable,
police tape squaring-off the surrogate chalk lines
he was; she was; they were.
And they were
still they. Albeit a faint tracing. Shadows
of snowberries on snow. A fogbraid
ghosting upriver between banks
opposite the current—

To be broken is to search for an image that will not
correspond to your brokenness and fail
at every turn: the boy's shoulders, even, burnished
in candlelight, become
such small bones
to bear such,
his pliant voice two rooms removed
becomes—
A little wind, though, and all the aspen catkins
lean one way, a single pilgrim bud poised as if it might
say something. Anything.
Hold me like I'm small.

*

More than a nick. Not the glasscut-moon

                     healing into midday sky,

but the valley's scar, vein-blue and unstitchable, where mule deer gather

to drink and regard their reflections, waning

in the waning dark, before mistaking parking ramp

for foothill—

               they reach the third-level roof in full light, frantic:

leap to the hoods, the windshields.

                        Who tends

these chambers full of fury, male anger at being born into a world

he can't control and thus tries harder to, the general rage

spilling over onto the snowbound playground:

                       the girls

fashioning a small snowbrick igloo, while the boys

thrash at each other's fortresses, turning

cheese slices into guns, pinecones into grenades that will

blow your guts all over this field.

                    She's bathing him—born

without birthmark, with all his fingers, two eyes, and his toes,

with an anus (they check for that), with openings

nine-fold to the world, and a slight vein

bridging his nose—

               in the sink, and with a plastic cup

pouring a thin rope of water into the basin below,

predicate light climbing,

descending the strand.

                He's passing his hand through it.

   *

If you think a witch's tit is cold
you've never been to Wolf Point in winter—

                      even the silos' shadows
freeze. The cold draws you
into yourself and it gets downright intimate.

                      Quick-dark, spur-stars
wheeling night along, the gone sun friendless, turning
down the covers, readying its room—

                 some late bird calling
even though.

   *

A road of thank-you-ma'ams, rut-forced nods

                 down to the river,
the final card, which was, once they reached it
all everyone had said it would be.

               Open your window,
hear that bird singing? (Sound of rain, pensive,
filling day's carafe, furtive wind in burdocks)

                then a few watery notes
like it had swallowed someone's keys and couldn't quite
spit them up:

       That's a call, not a song.

There's a difference?

Call's shorter, lacks a particular pattern. Listen (rifflesound
seined through branches, curr of the world disappearing, day's flame
snuffed)
        then the soaked air doused
with six shrill notes—
             I hear song.

   *

Deep-winter, the river a spill of ink.
                 Match-flare of morning
held to the boy, five months, smiling at white rice paper
inked with kanji figures:
             six strokes say
"mother and child." Shadows of his eyelashes
                    on his eyes—

   *

He wrote some lines to his life
             but had to sketch himself
a map to deliver them
You're going to have to let the moose crossing
the moiling current so that its reed-hidden calf can suckle
be a moose
        and not stand for something else,
let hooves stabbing for purchase between stones
be hooves, moss-black, or she won't get there—

Cloud, let what passes through you—swift song keening
against granite, the yellowthroat's *witchity-witchity-which,*
that last immeasurable, rain from far away—pass through,

the sawblades, too, of broken glass from the self's
smashed bottles, drowning water filling dreams, and light

                                                all the way from the moon
on the disbelieving cliffs.

                        Took so long an instant getting here.
No longer the net he thought he was, tangled
with six-pack plastic, a diving sea-bird's wing, he lifts
to horizon something scantly resembling himself,

                                the emptiness pearling.

    *

Red gash of dogwoods
The canyon's wolfish shade
Light-whiskered curve of ridgeline

                    Stand here, and let the eye ascend—

Deft as she was with the female form the painter never quite mastered hands.
So learned to immerse them in bath water, the shoal-like
folds of sheets. And still—

                    near to still as the living get, turn a circle
                    slow as your sun-dial-double's, try to find a line
                    among the rancorless peaks that doesn't recall—

almost shyly, the watercolors and huge oil canvases
sold. Flourished, some said, because—

                            undrastic, two lunate basins
                            beneath fusiform caps of snow
                            scintillant collarbone of clifftop—
she knew what to leave out.

(Despite cartoon depictions the formlessness of the heart which cannot contain
what passes through it and thus)

    *

As to why the new ceiling joists kept creaking, the carpenter
(they called him by his last name now, Ibison) had no theories
though on marriage he was level-sure that a *40-year-old woman*
should marry a 17-year-old man so that when the man is 40
the woman will be 73 and the man
can marry a 17-year-old woman.
                            Last-hour, the hills
ligneous in mitered light, his saws and stacked buckets
mere props: *By now,* he often began, gesturing
wildly with an unlit cigarette, *by now I've said*
too much, but . . .
                     —she watched instead the crows'
too-heavy half-finished fir-twig nest
high in the cottonwood, abandoned by its builders,
nodding, the phyll in deep flex—
                         inevitably something about the room's

energy, dependent on its unused space

                        —above the old neighbor couple's

window, their shades already drawn: they'd seen circus tents

staked where the garage now stood, elephants

watered at the hydrant, a trapeze girl fall

from that tree—

                his omnivorous voice finally idling, . . . *because isn't*

what we really love just form?

                     —Theirs: passing between

what must be an antique lamp and the window, clumsily,

as if they're moving furniture, an end table. Or perhaps

dancing.

Epithalamium

They lay down where the deer had lain, where the doe with its buck fawn pressed sage
into a bed, where in winter its musk melted snow. Where once she found a coyote's
skull into whose dead ears she whispered names of boys she'd loved and over which
birds passed and shadows of birds she knew by the sunmade mark of them on earth,
by call or wing-tinged wind above: meadowlark, golden eagle, harrier, though she sat
the half-broke piebald mare and thought *air-swimmers untouchable free* and dug
the horse out again. Afterward, horizon's hillocks lay like the spent, reclining bodies
they were and she asked *do not our hearts burn deep within us?* And though it twisted
hidden through canyon folds below, he felt the river pressed upon him and asked *what
is the test of a river? to kill a man,* they knew by heart and said. And awoke again at
day's hilt, crepuscular, the first star partially submerged in the sky like the tick seated
in the cleft behind her ear.

Rex's Georgic: Hunting Morels in Last Year's Burn

White whorls, three flags of trillium splash up from charred
ground. A ponderosa's boiled sap. Sometimes even in the spring
even after the long snows you can find a trunk still smoldering.

Puckett, you are the worst goddamn mushroom hunter I ever saw.
Like some drive-by mushroom hunter. Look: Slug always finds
his 'shroom.

Crow-caw. Crow-mew. Wind from far away. Crow-bark. Wind
in the dead chimes of the aspen.

Some folks'll rub soot on their face for luck. Paint warrior-lines
and such but it ain't about luck 't all. Matter of fact you know
Chick Alexander? Judge. Lost his son Abe when their baseball
rolled under the porch. Right in front of you. Next to your foot.

Swallowtails, cabbage-whites, the dark scat of denning wolves.
Little azures that love the dung.

So Abe goes digging after the ball and unwraps a den of young rattlers.
Thirty-seven bites. And that's countin'. You do know
Chick, right? Yeah, well he's a helluva mushroom hunter.

Dead deer. Button-buck. The difference between thistles
and burrs. What the dead do is none of our business.

That swale there's brimful of ticks so watchit. Had a ladyfriend once send me all these tick drawings after she left. She was thinking about me still. Said I was a tick under her skin.

Six swift clouds. Could enough of them erode a mountain.

Nope, I've never found 'em on that hill, though I did find fifteen pounds of weed growing there one year. No buds. But back then a leaf would get you high. You just stepped on one. Other boot.

Sundogs, two of them. A whole hillside of trillium. Roots the Nez Perce used to boil to arouse their sleeping lovers.

Now I have heard that before. Knew a couple tried it once. Fucked so long and hard their short hairs knotted.

That? That's a glacier lily. You can eat those. Watch.

Direction

Fireflies, those brief
untraceable scars, appear
early in the noon-
stabbed dusk, dark
that staggers onto stage
holding its neck.
What blood. Beneath
and by which the boy
can read the name she's
writing on his chest
with crushed bugs: one
for each letter as
the night grows large
around them. No,
the night grows large
and has nothing to do
with them yet. Old
palimpsest, ink
of our excuses, if ever
the boy no more
a boy returns, direction-
less, heeding each
momentary beacon,
walking his childhood
dog whose face has
grown so white and

with its black tear
so Auguste—if ever
he comes looking
for this place, page
of his old self, let him
run his fingers over
something vanished,
some way it takes
the dark to see.

Study for the Ridgeline Blue in Winter

Throbs up from the darkening draws, eluding
dusk's clutch. Calls out and the owl
calls back, answering with her own ample koan.
When the world was flat we thought darkness
fell. Now we know it rises firelike from earth,
spindling up the oaks' trunks, engulfing
ridge and canopy.
                         The resulting smoke, then—
hue of a breath exhaled by a late-arriving disciple
come to examine the charred chaos of day
(such a staunch monk!) igniting itself again—
the odorless remains.
                         Then. The hanging
particulate (try not to breathe it in). A mute coyote's
coat flecked with snow. Clear, cold-drawn
tear. Two children escaping with the last
unshattered mirror. Signals from which they send
to no one all night—no, no one—until dawn.

Heron Rookery Aubade

Above the Bitterroot and where the Bitterroot
swelled with sediment will run in early May,
and where the river in the flood of '47 chased
bawling cows, rafts of uprooted willow, once-
bridges, -roofs, -porchswings, with more volume
than ever, yet quiet;
                    above the alluvial scars,
cobbles shaped like prehistoric eggs, grasses
ruffed like crest-feathers by wind—high in the
cottonwoods' grasp of sky,
                    there: the nests
wide as the kitchen table a man sits at, upstream,
writing his lover a note: there is nothing to say.
He has ceased looking up to her, their rooms
have become the place of neck-bent solitudes,
of standing so long the feet tire. It is early enough
in the day to see these things,
                    early enough
in the season: bright tapestry of boulders
before the melt. Before the trees exhale their
one green breath and the bird unfolds
its wings—quiet as one who leaves his house
this morning, thinking she's still asleep.

Woodkate, Hackmatack

Story-high in the hackmatack, a woodkate
stands parallel to trunk, eyeing its work
then siring the shards of sound I've tracked
to this precise place beside the creek, where I
look up and the redmasked face looks down,
pulp falling from the hole like spits of hail
that just now start to fall—

                             the head
holds its hammer back and listens
for whatever grubs it sensed inside the marrow:
barkbeetle larvae, worms white as sleet-turned-snow,
soundless as snow vanishing in folds of creek
that vanish brightly the moment they become.

While the creek takes its time, meandering
out of sight the way a dialect disappears from language,
privy or not to its own distinction. So that anymore
to say *woodkate* or *hackmatack* is to hold
a former way of life in the mouth,
which is to hold what was in the body—

                                     breath,
snow, glimpse of light between the larches, drum
of unseen beak on wood. Brief undulating
flight of what is and is gone.

Motherless Children (Traditional)

"motherless children have a hard time crying"

Invisible atop the church spire: the rain elided cross
the boy in his hand-me-down trenchcoat looks back for
one last time, wind on his wet face and high & even
in the thick-chested willows, wind her last words
whispered and carried like a coin a pocketful of years
will rub smooth,

               and what can he buy with it now?
old snow? dust from a gypsy moth's wings, a cricket
swaddled in wolfspider web.

                  Her face by now
unseeable: eighteen years. And he can't even let a moose
crossing the thin August river be a moose, wants it
to stand for something else—for what?, some
leech-laden passage between this world and

                        that was what
she whispered, ultimately, that the unforgivable is to
forget that you are here. So don't: this comes back, entering
a box canyon recognizable only by cliff-shade filling it
in the exact moment when the fisherman, parched, bonetired,
arrives, and knows where he is.

                  Late-shine, the day tendered.
Caddis ovipositing on the shallow pool he kneels in (mascara
around her eyes like they'd rubbed fluttering wings

across her skin) cups hands to drink from. And who

stares up from his reflection, whose face is it, anyway,

falling through his fingers.

Self-Portrait as Dandelion Head Discovered in the Crop of a Partridge

Pomp among the grain and barley seeds, two hardened
kernels of corn, the caul-like brain-gray bag packed tight: luminous dream
snapped-off before its denouement.
                                        A piece of him?—
she used to pick the lucky caps and yellow-up her breasts
till they drew bees. Stung once on the lip he was.
                                        Joint-laborer
with goshawk, flushed the covey back and forth (ever seen
a shadow fall?)
                    Traversed the vast landscape
of the formerly keen slowly closing eye, closed it with his thumb:
a buff corona around the lid, crown of feathers, bloody
crown of thorns. Peeled plumage back from breast. Cut in,
coroner with inside information.
                                        Stood in a long unscarred wind
scattering the faintly fragrant seeds, desperate for the meadow's coronation.

Aftersketch for

"Self-Portrait as Dandelion Head Discovered in the Crop of a Partridge"

The pedicel was waxy enough to draw with, wooling at the roots, and I kept wanting to say *Mama had a baby and his head popped off* but that seemed obvious as a head on a platter, the Baptist's head, blood spilling over the gold rim and caking in his long curls (as in Titian's version), Salome looking downwardly askance at the head her mother had asked for after the girl's dance provoked so deep an arousal in Herod that, drunk, hard, he offered to honor her any request, or by turns, by default, her mother's: Herodias, married to her brother-in-law-of-old, who despised all critics of her marriage, among them John: who is most often portrayed seated next to a lamb or pointing toward the sky, who would've eaten the dandelion head discovered in the crop and likely the still-kicking grasshoppers I've found on other occasions. John who said he'd seen who he'd said was coming. Was sure of it. His prophecies. Who among the us that I am can say as much? Head on a platter or not.

Van Gogh's Palette

Grey of a still spiderweb, the spider, unglistening
grayish-green, sleeping at its center; quick-blue
of a girl's winked eye, a curious lantern's cadmium
flaring on the pupil; invisible white of wind
through predawn wheat, swart-white of gulls
ascending the same; pitchy brown of eyes closed
for untold intervals, all the brief-orange sunspots
vanished; frost-stained tan of fence posts; cream
like almond centers, like parings of cloud;
silver of dew on a sickle yoked across
a young man's shoulders; open-wound
red, gauze-stain ochre, salmon of itchy scabs,
rust of waterlines in bathtubs; purplish blooming-
black of brief tiresome sleeps; forgotten black
of the womb: dark where we were, dark
where we're going, and this is the sunlight—

A History of Barbed Wire

I.

In the beginning Rose
drove the spikes into
a strip of wood, then strapped
the prickered board to
the head of a breachy cow,
thinking, thus armed, the cow
would mind the fences.

* * *

Dekalb County Fair, 1872.
Behind the booth selling Sally Smitts'
rhubarb pie, the Elwood boy leads
the cornshucking contest by six ears.
Rita Elwood pulls her husband Ike aside,
whispers under the din: "Well, at least
we'll take home one blue ribbon tonight—
that Glidden fence was better than yours."
Ike wanders out alone, into the wire tent
where his yellow ribbon tied to the table
kicks and settles in the breeze.
Behind the tent, the same breeze
chases leaves across the lawn, pins
sticks and paper bags to the picket
surrounding the park, the girl
swinging in her swing—*Hello, Wind,*

she cries, holding tightly to the chains,
Good-bye, good-bye—

      * * *

Playing baseball with the dead, I stand
between rows of alfalfa, pitching
stones to a one-armed batter, his bat
a long thin branch of willow that quivers
in his hand. For the light, he can't see
the small stones coming. I mix it up:
a pebble low and away, a brush-back,
one fist-sized rock down the pipe. *Strike-called,*
the blind ump says, *Swing and a miss.*
In the stands the crowd is singing.

    II.

At dawn, looking down the rifle barrel
at a scrawny fawn: first whistling shot
plugs fence post, bounds her off
across the breaks. Through the scope
I watch her at the wire, curled
in question: over? under? through?
What is it? Perhaps Scott's Cocked
Rings, Upham's Loop and Lock?
Or Jayne Hill's Barb, Ford's Kink
and Double Twist—I knew an old timer
who strung Forrester's Sawtooth Blade,
and once, Phillips' Hollow Cocklebur.
This numb sound of wind-bent wire

is like a stare: some afternoons
a southeast gust makes the whole pasture
hum. The dead do not watch or sing.

*   *   *

Ike Elwood said to Glidden: "If I
get it patented will you give me
half of all we make from it?"
"Well, Ike, I hadn't allowed to
make anything from it, just
to keep those dat-ratted pigs
out of the garden."

*   *   *

And the lovers, picking chokecherries in the marsh,
tufts of cattail loosed in the wind like plumage,
down, postscript to last night's swan-slaughter
seen through binoculars from the hill: seven
coyotes, two distracted swans, the ambush
frightening, beautifully white. Walking back
with bucketfuls and hands quick with slivers,
she's talking about a former lover's fingers, of all
the ways to forget them.

III.

Late that evening, fence line fastened
to fence line shadow, willows
footed to darkening shapes
in the ford, on a green scrap
of paper, I draw the best horse

I've ever drawn. She's staring
over her roan shoulder, into
unsketched fields, wind
folding and unfolding her mane, riffling
through another meadow of her life.

    * * *

Then the ghost of the boy whose wallet
I found along the Big Hole River
must have heard me going through his things,
peeling dollar bills apart, reading
the note from Sylvia who'd written, *Call me, don't be shy:*

    * * *

I had no idea water
could get this cold
without freezing November
the shelf ice stacks up
the fishermen quit coming
I miss the sound of the gravel
their boots kicked loose
its clack and shuffle
along the cobble
how I could hear it long
after it tumbled out of sight
most nights a dozen
deer stop to drink
their anvil hooves
punching through the ice
arriving on the black

mat of leaves in a silent
explosion it sounds
strange but I can sense
each inch of water
the river loses as they lap
so when tonight they drank
too long I reached out
and tapped a skinny foreleg
startling the herd into
the river's thrust dangling
legs a yearling's neck
and spotted flank
they forded weightless
flightlike fearless of
the other shore once
I spooked a great
horned owl
from its rook inside
a juniper those slow
wings opened broad
as a man hoisted it
above the alkali grounded
it could have been
a buddha and hanging
exposed a christ
but when I throttled
through the sage it simply
settled in beside

the truck and coasted there
awhile companion
before kicking off
into the darkness a long
while I sat in the sand-stalled
truck listening for some
sure sign of the bird
light thud of vole
dropped to the ground
some barb of wire catching
the owl's wing at
the edge of the world
but heard nothing
which is what I heard
for months until
the dogwoods peeled
open and I heard
their leaf music the river
under sun under
stars its song
increasing toward
morning until
only it is audible

Late Evening Fugue

From here the grazing horse's eye is glass,
and the hummingbird's beak a bridge the horse

must cross. I fear the sleep of dogs, wind-twitch
beneath bones, the sound of shallow water

rising toward an ear; each bead of sap hanging
from the buds' tongue tips. Like storytellers

the last drops of daylight shimmering in the cottonwoods
have a kind of generosity I can't muster tonight. I picked

the buds and boiled them into the fragrant syrup he once
rubbed under my nose, saying gruffly, "Don't forget"—

but I've misplaced the pillbox I poured the syrup in.
My grandfather thought death was like

arriving at a motel room so exhausted
that everything wrong with the room seemed fine,

sufficient: the fan's erratic seizing, the faucet
dripping its cool slaver down the drain,

the starched white sheet not quite reaching
your neck. Dawn, the meadowlark calls, and you're

not quite awake. Not quite asleep. Did I say
the creek gets louder the later it gets, that waves

dance like lit fuses, and all night banks inhale?
This is the kind of passage we often attempt: hoof

balanced on twig; all the air the lungs can hold;
the first word waiting patiently to fail. Once, in fall, I found

a monarch butterfly frozen under the porch steps, and waited
for my grandfather to climb down from the semi-truck,

watching as he tried first with his fingers, then with a jack-knife,
to keep the vellum wings intact—he touched his crude

tongue to the bulb of ice that held the fragile legs
like fossils . . . If I told you what became of the butterfly

I would have to give it to you, would have to give you
so many things I've loved and gathered up, pockets filled

with waspnest scraps, osier bark, all the moon-shaped stones.
The bridge-makings. Things fragile and serene: the horse's eye

in which lies cupped the sky and washing trees,
my own nearing face.

The Flu, the Bath

Maybe it was the fence-post-perched meadowlark
splashing its song through the evening air just after Torey's
shot in *Shane,* tiny gouts of blood blooming
in rain-filled wagon tracks; or the way the doctor
met my eyes, only in the mirror, as I coughed up
what felt like bits of glass; or Kurosawa's bandit
swordsman itching, a moment before he strikes
the final blow, a mosquito bite:
$\qquad\qquad\qquad\qquad\qquad$ I don't know what
assured me my death would be so forgettable, just
as we can't know the exact cause of a flu, walking
pneumonia. I drew the bath I thought I might
and knew I wouldn't die in—outside waxwings
had vanished from the branches, no one to knell
for me—and after some time had to pee, tried
with wet palms to lift myself from the tub, quavering
shoulders. From inside the hair shining like seaweed,
it breached the water's surface: its little eye or mouth
releasing a thin invisible fluid that rippled the bath,
breath blown over a cup of tea to cool it.
$\qquad\qquad\qquad\qquad\qquad\qquad$ Where does
prayer come from. Warbled notes, glance, cold hand
reaching down to clasp a shoulder in the bath—
$\qquad\qquad\qquad\qquad\qquad\qquad$ remind me I am here.

Runt Puppies in the Shade under the Porch

They are the neighbor's or the neighbor's neighbor's,
but mostly they are
                      this brief homily from the gospel
according to June:
                   the air, after week-old sheepdogs roll
through wild vetch, smells of wild vetch, the scent
first-tooth sharp, puncturing warm air that weeks ago
(Fun Country's waterslide snowed in like a cruel joke)
seemed a preposterous hope—
                          but winter
fills summer's buckets, and here was here before
we were with our gingham, beer and rhubarb crisp
tasting precisely this tart because dogs peed
near the stems, scrapped, or lay briefly spent inside
foliate spills of shade. Milk-tongues dangling
                             as they are
now, flanks heaving, the cool dark divvied
by thinnest ribs of light.

Hunting All Day beneath the Long Night Moon

until it seems time is told on the handless face

noon-reflected in creekwater trying

to slow its descent through the valley, the outhills

under hoarfrost white and pure as death

                                       rarely is: the pheasant's beak

full of the nightshade it dropped into

like a puppet abandoned by its master's hands—

                                               What of you

will last in me who knows not how or whom to ask,

(in orison?) world or regal bird

                            nor what carves us, knifeless,

from shivering limbs.

Whittling

Boy with blades, I sharpened sticks
to blades. Now this idleness is my act
of aggression, the furled cedar shavings
falling into the pile of shavings that is
the hour the world wants most from me—
how about this hummingbird instead:
what was in the wood before I found it
swirling in an eddy's foam, drew the blade
on it, over it, until tail feathers splayed open,
a long, needle beak tilted down as if
to drink. This is as close to nothing
as I can do and love the time
it takes, so long I often apologize to
the bird who must get bored—it takes
time I say which is the truth which is
never dull even when what's true
seems commonplace. Like when a child
pressing his head against your chest says
it sounds like something tapping
on the cabin window.

Wind's Heroics

Whereas the long shadows of wires part our chance communions,
the wind, bled of all color, comes wending in to reconcile;

Westerly, it speaks for no one, swirling inside a bus-stop eddy
like a tract heralding a savior we've already missed;

As to its next incarnation, it appears while unseen ambivalent,
or at least too busy steering great rafts of clouds to comment;

A svaha, we wager, *breath blown across a dead dog's water bowl,*
smart-money in early on *luminist of Dakota wheat;*

Shunning accompaniment, it remains in ubiquity, staunch
in its fasting, in its sacrifice, as an American attack;

See it, in the unwashed skylight, jostling the fallen
leaves, in the finch-cracked window the cliques of berries;

How great you are, we say, *how great,* mendicants at ballgames
begging it to stop a deep shot midair—how rote of us;

Failing to elicit even one of its myriad expressions, how ignorable
we are, how unlike two red-shafted flickers mating atop a phone pole:

One of whose shrill-orange feathers it gently shoulders to the ground;
carrying no judgment, it has more arms for courage, more arms

for us than we could number, than even the lab tech, ciphering
each creature's lifetime count of heartbeats at two billion, could tally.

O Stethoscope, so cold on our bare chests, this great Niagara
you must hear, determine it, as we have not, interminable.

Epithalamium

Like the hair she has waited all day to let down,
a shadow unfurls from the ponderosa's trunk: a plank
one might walk to horizon's edge, the dark band
just stops.
      And out there,
                a fractured school of minnows
veering all at once, gulls belly-up and disappear
in dunegrass.
        Like doubloons, gills, like rusted keys,
or the first glimpse of shore, comparisons
fail: *She's a splinter in the general noon;*
a stalled grain on which he stands, he is in no way
sure.
    And still the branches sway like a chorus
of believers: arms urging the moored ship off,
years-later waves washing them into the salt
of what was there.

Koan

What is leaf-shade on rock? is a question that has comforted
and confounded since we were clambering
down sharp slopes in the Missions last evening, falling in a way
toward a falling sun. I saw the shadow—
a flock of cowbirds lighting in field of cut-wheat, waves rising
warningless from a still pond—before I saw
its maker, an aspen missing half its leaves, because for balance
I have to watch my feet. Something I had said
hurt you, and now we were alternate sides of the earth, midnight
and noon: in my ecstasy I even looked up to thank
the sun for finding this tree, the tree this stone its canvas,
while you sat hunched on a boulder saying
keep going, I'll catch up. As you would. As sorrow—unfathomable
velocity!—always catches up with joy, or vice versa:
so that this morning it does not surprise me to find you sunlit
on the porch feeding rosehips to the cat, batting her paw
away. Sometimes at certain heights or depths in this life together
I have understood a oneness as transparent
and as baffling. Your hand opens, reveals a rosehip. No, thank you.
No? you ask, *what is it?*

Landscape with Scavengers and Bonelight

All day the ravens shit the buck whitetail
back onto his antlers, the thick arcing tines
graffitied with undigested tendons. Coyote-
dragged, draped in a squawking garment
that rises tattered when redtail-harried—
revealing ribs, links of spine, tongue-clean
sockets—and falls, in patches, back, stitched
with wingsound. A feathered hush. Says you will

go down in the dirt. First the four-leggeds
ferrying your shape across the slough, yipping
nothing resembling a name, large birds then like

lamp-drawn moths, before the six-limbed elders
arrive as one mind, as shifting soil, to polish
what's left, forsaking only the inedible brain.

Elegy with Fall's Last Filaments

In the one world
you called twin
tired of being
misidentified how
swiftly you became
the spider mending
each day its
wind-rent web and not
the box-elder beetle you
had been grasshopper
still tearing
at the ties intricate void
bright bardo room
she I call her hangs
like a home light
beneath the eaves and you
would have left her on

All kinds of kindnesses
Luka just two
at noon yesterday
where'd the moon go
daddy   The neighbors'
plums landing ripely
in our lawn Portrait
of you as webstrand

stretched between
the fences Sky-
deep lake appearing
halfway into my hike
as if it knew I were
thirsty—sat down
sketched the swale
in one broad stroke
fainter lines for where
the fog had hung
and almost asked
if you'd found
a formlessness yet
didn't—tempting
to pick a few
forget-me-knots
marking the soundless
rill

Stir a little
shallows with your
alderleaf archipelagos
branch and cloud
reflections drawn
so crisply I mistake
one white trunk for
the other   Stir
a little sawdust

from the just cut
deadfall firewood
tepeed now above
the tinder I light
before shucking
my shirt and jeans—
things *little soul little*
stray you used to make
fun of these the last
words you quoted me
asking *now where*
will you stay?
—and plunging
through the cold lake
body strung with quick-
silver sunlight leaking down
to fill escaping orbs
of air gone as you are
probably no one
joins anyone here or after
you said but perhaps
the silence we've
always expected from
the dead isn't
exactly silence

On surfacing
you want to have

something warm
to sit by tidy
fire tsk-tsking
this entire notion
but easing away
the gooseflesh
the body's automatic
response

Hiking out
plucked from a steaming
pile of blackbear scat
a huckleberry still whole
skin unblemished
large pupil in the
vitreous of my palm
who's watching
mote-midges blurring
through fruitless stems
unadorned lady-
bugs imago mayflies
the illustrious bound for webs
orbiting each other fall's
last filaments
kept thinking
law versus spirit
what we're told
versus what we're

told—no one no
spring to rinse
the fruit only
a watering mouth

ACKNOWLEDGMENTS

"Get Up, John" is the title of a bluegrass tune composed by Bill Monroe; the poem borrows a phrase from Robert Penn Warren's *Audubon: A Vision*.

"October Suite" is indebted to Jim Harrison's suites.

When the carpenter-voice speaks in the last section of "Some Nights the River," he's cribbing from Charles Olson, who said "One loves only form, and form only comes into existence when a thing is born."

"A History of Barbed Wire" gathers much of its historical information and anecdotes from *Barbs, Prongs, Points, Prickers, and Stickers* by Robert T. Clifton (University of Oklahoma Press, 1970).

"Elegy with Fall's Last Filaments" is for Patricia Goedicke and converses with her poem "Night Notes"; the italicized passage is from "Little Soul" (after Hadrian) by W. S. Merwin.

Many thanks to the following journals, in which some of these poems previously appeared:

Alligator Juniper: "A History of Barbed Wire"
Barrow Street: "More than a nick" (from "Some Nights the River")
Basalt: "Self-Portrait as Dandelion Head Discovered in the Crop of a Partridge,"
    "Aftersketch for 'Self-Portrait as Dandelion Head Discovered in the Crop of a Partridge'"
Bloomsbury Review: "Direction"
Colorado Review: "Rex's Georgic: Hunting Morels in Last Year's Burn"
Crazyhorse: "October Suite"
Del Sol Review: "Hunting All Day beneath the Long Night Moon"
Denver Quarterly: "Midst"
Green Mountains Review: "Boreal," "To Carry Water"
Louisville Review: "Late Evening Fugue," "The Flu, the Bath"
Luna: "Bullethole"

Neo (Portugal): "Poem Beginning and Ending with Haiku"

Ninth Letter: "Some Nights the River"

Poetry: "Get Up, John," "Landscape with Scavengers and Bonelight"

Orion: "Epithalamium"

Salt Hill: "Fragments with Dusk in Them"

Talking River Review: "Heron Rookery Aubade," "Woodkate, Hackmatack"

Tar River Poetry: "Koan"

"The Flu, the Bath" was reprinted in *Joyful Noise: An Anthology of American Spiritual Poetry* (Autumn House, 2006).

"Elegy with Fall's Last Filaments" was reprinted in *Making Poems* (SUNY Press, 2009).

"October Suite" was reprinted in *Poems Across the Big Sky* (Many Voices Press, 2007).

"Get Up, John," "Fragments with Dusk in Them," "Rex's Georgic: Hunting Morels in Last Year's Burn," and "Elegy with Fall's Last Filaments" also appeared on The Fishouse: An Audio Archive of Emerging Poets (www.fishousepoems.org).

Some of these poems previously appeared in *Fragments with Dusk in Them*, a limited edition chapbook from Punctilious Press (2008).

My abiding gratitude to: Jim Colando, Michael Delp, Alexander Deussen, Peter Drake, David Duncan, Michael Eastman, Patricia Goedicke, the Matthew Hansen Endowment, Joanna Klink, Tobias Lawrence, Mary McGinn, Matthew McGinn, Jefferson Miller, Mason Miller, Greg Pape, Nicholas Popoff, Sam Reed, Jack Ridl, John Roberts, Rob Schlegel, Deborah Slicer, Caroline Temple, University of Montana, Miles Waggener, Daniel Webster. Thank you to my family for their immense support. And to my mother and father, and to Luca and Molly, for inspiration and sustenance.